T0067092

RESTORATION

Restoring Relationship

CHARLES WHITE

authorHOUSE®

AuthorHouse™
1663 Liberty Drive
Bloomington, IN 47403
www.authorhouse.com
Phone: 1 (800) 839-8640

Published by AuthorHouse 01/30/2015

ISBN: 978-1-4969-6799-2 (sc)
ISBN: 978-1-4969-6798-5 (e)

Contents

About the Book

This book was clearly influenced by God's Holy Spirit, to break down a well known scripture (Matthew 22:37), in giving strategic information on restoring our relationship with the father.

Introduction

This book was clearly influenced by God's Holy Spirit, to break down a well known scripture Matthew 22:37, in giving strategic information on restoring our relationship with the father. It challenges the reader to focus on his/her, mind, heart and will. This book will not only challenge but strengthen the remaining or existing relationship with the Father. It's soul purpose is to restore a fading generation that's driven off of lies and hypocrisies, implemented by false leaders in today's church. I plan to tear down the walls of heresy, and restore the unadulterated word of God in every believer life. I hope this reading becomes a blessing to all who engages it. Be blessed in Jesus name amen...

PART 1

Restoring our mind to God:
Chapter 1 Renewing our Mind

Romans 12:1 I beseech you therefore, brethren, by the mercies of God, that ye present your bodies a living sacrifice, holy, acceptable unto God, [which is] your reasonable service.

2 And be not conformed to this world: but be ye transformed by the renewing of your mind, that ye may prove what [is] that good, and acceptable, and perfect, will of God.

Paul started off by saying, "I beg you". This adds an importance to the message he wanted to share. He follows it by adding, "by the mercies of God". Paul begged man to restore their minds. He wanted us to renew our minds, which means there was a different state or mindset given to man before.

The word renew means: to resume an activity after interruption; to recommit or validate an expiring contract.

In other words, somewhere down the line our mindset was interrupted, causing an expiring contract. It is our job to find out where this interruption is in our lives. In order to do so we must do a trouble shoot, to check for issues. In order to resume the mind we must look at what the mind is. The mind is defined as, the element of a person that enables them to be aware of the world and their experiences, to think, and to feel; the faculty of consciousness and thought. It is a power of conscious and thought, knowledge and intellectual thinking. This power was given to us in genesis chapter three.

Genesis 3:4 And the serpent said unto the woman, Ye shall not surely die:

5 For God doth know that in the day ye eat thereof, then your eyes shall be opened, and ye shall be as gods, knowing good and evil.

6 And when the woman saw that the tree [was] good for food, and that it [was] pleasant to the eyes, and a tree

to be desired to make [one] wise, she took of the fruit thereof, and did eat, and gave also unto her husband with her; and he did eat.

7 And the eyes of them both were opened, and they knew that they [were] naked; and they sewed fig leaves together, and made themselves aprons. 3:22 And the LORD God said, Behold, the man is become as one of us, to know good and evil: and now, lest he put forth his hand, and take also of the tree of life, and eat, and live for ever:

It was here where Adam and Eve was given a mindset. They became aware of their nakedness and surrounding situations. They gained a power of consciousness and thought. Now knowing good and evil, their conscious began to speak to their thoughts. Knowing they disobeyed, caused a shame on themselves, leading them to take action and hide. Before eating the fruit they had no knowledge of good and evil, just the direct order of God. His commands was their thought process. In eating the fruit something happened. Disobedience became the interruption in activity causing a need of renewal. It altered the the contract of God, leaving man with a choice, rather than relying on God himself. This was not the divine will of God. This interruption in communication is still rapid in the world today. We have mind interruptions all the time. Usually these interruptions are foolish and unnecessary. Man must restore that divine connection with God by getting rid of these interruptions in order to renew our mind. The key to this reconnecting is obedience.

Proverbs 3:6 In all thy ways acknowledge him, and he shall direct thy paths.

Matthew <u>6:33</u> But seek ye first the kingdom of God, and his righteousness; and all these things shall be added unto you.

These scriptures guide us back to the mindset of depending on God. See Adam listened to the voice of God on a continual basis, this is the connection we should have. He never made a move outside of the voice of God. If we begin to acknowledge The Lord in all our ways we will begin to see that connection between God and man. If we choose not to, we'll continue to see an expiring contract throughout our lives. Our health will expire, our finances will expire, our joy will expire, our peace will expire, and even life itself will eventually expire. Leaving us in a state of a fading glory against God's promising eternal life. We must take the power gained by us in the garden, to identify our surroundings in this world and include God into its experiences. These steps will begin a renewal process in our life, restoring the breach in activity and expanding the contract of eternal life. The key is to resume the activity of total dependency in God. This may take a level of faith that we're not use to. Long periods of time we've become accustomed to doing things our way, or in our strength, but that has to end in order to get back to our first state of mind. Let us work diligently to accomplish this renewal process in Jesus name we pray, Amen.

Restoring our mind to God: Chapter 2 Let This Mind

Philippians 2:1 If [there be] therefore any consolation in Christ, if any comfort of love, if any fellowship of the Spirit, if any bowels and mercies,

2 Fulfil ye my joy, that ye be likeminded, having the same love, [being] of one accord, of one mind.

3 [Let] nothing [be done] through strife or vainglory; but in lowliness of mind let each esteem other better than themselves.

4 Look not every man on his own things, but every man also on the things of others.

5 Let this mind be in you, which was also in Christ Jesus:

This passage lets us know that we as Christians must be like minded sharing the same passion of love. It goes on to say, being of one accord, of one mind. Paul tell us that this singleness of mind was the same mindset that Christ had, and explains to us that we should share this way of thinking. In this chapter we will take a look at the mind Christ accepted, and it's roll in our lives. His willingness to become the sacrifice of love, to get all believers on the same page of faith. In accepting this mind it cost Christ His life. This is the sacrifice of giving we must accept. Giving until it hurts. Paul said that Christ became obedient to the point, that He was clothed in humility all the way to the grave. Even though the cross had nothing to do with the saving of himself, he embraced it for others. This is the highest act of self-denial we will ever see.

Matthew 16:24 Then said Jesus unto his disciples, If any [man] will come after me, let him deny himself, and take up his cross, and follow me.

Jesus says, "if any man is in pursuit of me, let him not think of himself but take his cross and follow what I did." In order to pursue you must follow. This is the only and true way to get the mind of Christ. Philippians 2:1 spoke of this like mindedness, to esteem others better than ourselves. The cross again is not just for you. It takes a level of humility to accomplish this act of love. To deny how you feel or what you feel for someone else. The mass of this message is self denial. Christ displayed this to the fullest. Taking on pounds of sin, to liberate us from the hands of the enemy. A lot of us take this too lightly. Jesus said who so ever shall find his life shall lose it. You only gain life when you give up yours for God (**Matthew 10:39**). In restoring our minds we have to remember that ministry is the first goal. Inside that ministry is self-denial. The word minister means: to attend to the wants and needs of others, or to serve. When God called us, this was his purpose. In **Genesis 1:26-28** God saw fit to make us ministers to all the earth. He called us to rule and subdue it through our relationship and dependence on him.

That word subdue means: to make subordinate, dependent, subservient.

Our jobs as ministers is to get the world unified with the mind of Christ. To usher them into a subordinate and dependent state of mind. All of this is a part of renewing our mindset. Subdue also means: to put down by force.

Matthew 11:12 (ASV) 12 And from the days of John the Baptist until now the kingdom of heaven suffereth violence, and men of violence take it by force.

Matthew 11:12 (NET) 12 From the days of John the Baptist until now the kingdom of heaven has suffered violence, and forceful people lay hold of it.

Matthew 11:12 (KJV) 12 And from the days of John the Baptist until now the kingdom of heaven suffereth violence, and the violent take it by force.

These scriptures explain that the kingdom is being attacked, Violently! God's unified mind for His body is being violently attacked. This is all do to the lack of subduing the world by changing our mindset. By not having a mind of his own Adam lost his kingdom on earth making satan the god of this world **(2nd Corinthians 4:4).** It is now our God's attempt to restore to us this world by bringing His kingdom on earth, through the unified mind of his people with Christ. This would take us back to the rightful place of us subduing the earth and subjecting satan's kingdom to transformation. If we do not embrace this mindset to subdue, we will never gain the authority God attended for us. This format of conquering comes through love. We must subdue/make dependent by love.

1st Peter 4:8 And above all things have fervent charity among yourselves: for charity shall cover the multitude of sins.

Peter states that charity/love covers a multitude of sins. This is the gateway to conquering, love. In order to gain our kingdom back, we must dominate with love. Love has to be a mindset. It has to be a continual way of thinking. David spoke of God having compassion five times in the book of Psalms. The gospels (Matthew, Mark, Luke & John), spoke of Jesus having compassion fourteen times **(King James Versions).** Jesus was also mentioned of being full of compassion. This is the same mind we must have just as Paul ushered us into in Philippians. Again let's seek this mind of charity, love and compassion, and become unified in it. I pray this by the strength of Christ Jesus. Amen.

Restoring our mind to God: Chapter 3 The Conscience

1st Timothy 4:1 Now the Spirit speaketh expressly, that in the latter times some shall depart from the faith, giving heed to seducing spirits, and doctrines of devils;

2 Speaking lies in hypocrisy; having their conscience seared with a hot iron;

Paul started of by saying the spirit is speaking Expressly! Meaning, he had specific instructions of what he wanted to say. He begins speaking about men falling away from the faith through seducing doctrines, they would later end up with a seared conscience. A lot of people now days have a seared conscience, meaning it is dead. In restoring our mind, we must revive that conscience, bringing it back to life again. In order to do this we must pray for a conviction from the Holy Spirit. We must ask God to convict us of all our evil, even in thought.

Psalms 139:23 Search me, O God, and know my heart: try me, and know my thoughts:

24 And see if [there be any] wicked way in me, and lead me in the way everlasting.

In this scripture David ask The Lord to, **"try me and know my thoughts".** Verse 24 he ask to check if any wicked way be in me, and change it. We have to get this same mindset toward our relationship with Christ. God has to examine us in order to convict us. Most of the time we don't wanna be examined because we know the evil of our hearts. Even when we're sick, we're afraid to go to the doctors office, because we don't wanna hear a negative report. Like wise, we take this same approach with God. We continue on in our lives, thinking we can somehow heal ourselves. What happens is we intentionally plan and carry out our devised evil against God, without considering His feelings towards us. Again in Timothy, Paul states some will depart by giving heed to seducing spirits and doctrines of devils.

To give heed means: to pay close attention to. The Greek definition (prosechō), means: to turn the mind to, to be attentive to and care for.

He said our minds will turn to seducing devils. Wow! **Romans 1:21-32**, talks about the evil of men and what's described as the end time signs. Verse 28 says God gave them over to a reprobate mind.

Reprobate *adokimos, Greek for,* that which does not prove itself as it ought. Another translation says a depraved mind. Meaning to turn away from what's morally right. When we lose our conscience and it becomes seared, we tend to become depraved. Especially when we pay attention to doctrine from devils. Verses 29-32, States:

Being filled with all unrighteousness, fornication, wickedness, covetousness, maliciousness; full of envy, murder, debate, deceit, malignity; whisperers,

30 Backbiters, haters of God, despiteful, proud, boasters, inventors of evil things, disobedient to parents,

31 Without understanding, covenant-breakers, without natural affection, implacable, unmerciful:

32 Who knowing the judgment of God, that they which commit such things are worthy of death, not only do the same, but have pleasure in them that do them.

If you have any symptom of what I just named, without conviction, you might have a seared conscience. Carefully read the list again. Boasters, covenant-breakers, backbiters all these are signs of a seared conscience. To boast about success, to brake a commitment, or talk about someone. All signs of a seared conscience. The only remedy is to become transformed by renewing the mind. Going back to acknowledging God in every area of our life. Pulling the curtain on this evil that we do behind the scenes and asking God to examine us, and change it. What makes us different from a sinner if we all have sin in our lives? The answer is the effort we put into changing the sin in our life. Starting with our conscience. See sinners, as explained in verse 32, not only do those sins, but take pleasure in doing them. If we, as Christians partake of those sins, our conscience will convict us leading to repentance. Having a repented heart allows mercy to come in and cover us while grace enters in and changes us.

2nd Corinthians 1:12 For our rejoicing is this, the testimony of our conscience, that in simplicity and godly sincerity, not with fleshly wisdom, but by the grace of God, we have had our conversation in the world, and more abundantly to you-ward.

This same Paul who stated in Romans that when I try to do good evil is present with me. Even calling himself a wretched man (**Romans 7:24**). Now states he's rejoicing over his testimony of his conscience, that by grace gave a good report in the world.

John 8:9 And they which heard [it], being convicted by [their own] conscience, went out one by one, beginning at the eldest, [even] unto the last: and Jesus was left alone, and the woman standing in the midst.

Acts 23:1 And Paul, earnestly beholding the council, said, Men [and] brethren, I have lived in all good conscience before God until this day.

Acts 24:16 And herein do I exercise myself, to have always a conscience void of offense toward God, and [toward] men.

These scriptures speak of how having a good conscience before God is important. John speaks of men who accused a woman, seeking to stone her. Later their conscience convicted them allowing them to walk away. Acts 23 Paul says he lived in all good conscience before God till that present day. Chapter 24 he explains, I exercise myself, to have a conscience void of offense toward God and man. Paul had to exercise a good conscience. It takes time to change your way of thinking, especially when the mind entertain hundreds of thoughts a day. This goes back to depending on God, and allowing him to format our mindset. I pray this section of this book challenged you to expand your mind in ways that will forever be pleasing before God. May we take the time to ask God to revive us from a seared conscience, and consider us once again. Amen!

Restoring our minds to God: Chapter 4 Recap

Romans 12:1 I beseech you therefore, brethren, by the mercies of God, that ye present your bodies a living sacrifice, holy, acceptable unto God, [which is] your reasonable service.

2 And be not conformed to this world: but be ye transformed by the renewing of your mind, that ye may prove what [is] that good, and acceptable, and perfect, will of God.

The word renew means: to resume an activity after interruption; to recommit or validate an expiring contract.

Genesis 3:4 And the serpent said unto the woman, Ye shall not surely die:

5 For God doth know that in the day ye eat thereof, then your eyes shall be opened, and ye shall be as gods, knowing good and evil.

6 And when the woman saw that the tree [was] good for food, and that it [was] pleasant to the eyes, and a tree to be desired to make [one] wise, she took of the fruit thereof, and did eat, and gave also unto her husband with her; and he did eat.

7 And the eyes of them both were opened, and they knew that they [were] naked; and they sewed fig leaves together, and made themselves aprons. 3:22 And the LORD God said, Behold, the man is become as one of us, to know good and evil: and now, lest he put forth his hand, and take also of the tree of life, and eat, and live for ever:

Proverbs 3:6 In all thy ways acknowledge him, and he shall direct thy paths.

Matthew 6:33 But seek ye first the kingdom of God, and his righteousness; and all these things shall be added unto you.

Philippians 2:1 If [there be] therefore any consolation in Christ, if any comfort of love, if any fellowship of the Spirit, if any bowels and mercies,

2 Fulfil ye my joy, that ye be likeminded, having the same love, [being] of one accord, of one mind.

3 [Let] nothing [be done] through strife or vainglory; but in lowliness of mind let each esteem other better than themselves.

4 Look not every man on his own things, but every man also on the things of others.

5 Let this mind be in you, which was also in Christ Jesus:

Matthew <u>16:24</u> Then said Jesus unto his disciples, If any [man] will come after me, let him deny himself, and take up his cross, and follow me.

Matthew <u>11:12</u> (ASV) 12 And from the days of John the Baptist until now the kingdom of heaven suffereth violence, and men of violence take it by force.

Matthew <u>11:12</u> (NET) 12 From the days of John the Baptist until now the kingdom of heaven has suffered violence, and forceful people lay hold of it.

Matthew <u>11:12</u> (KJV) 12 And from the days of John the Baptist until now the kingdom of heaven suffereth violence, and the violent take it by force.

1st Timothy 4:1 Now the Spirit speaketh expressly, that in the latter times some shall depart from the faith, giving heed to seducing spirits, and doctrines of devils;

2 Speaking lies in hypocrisy; having their conscience seared with a hot iron;

John 8:9 And they which heard [it], being convicted by [their own] conscience, went out one by one, beginning at the eldest, [even] unto the last: and Jesus was left alone, and the woman standing in the midst.

Acts 23:1 And Paul, earnestly beholding the council, said, Men [and] brethren, I have lived in all good conscience before God until this day.

Acts 24:16 And herein do I exercise myself, to have always a conscience void of offense toward God, and [toward] men.

PART 2

Restoring our hearts to God: Chapter 1 Evil of the heart.

Genesis 6:5 And GOD saw that the wickedness of man [was] great in the earth, and [that] every imagination of the thoughts of his heart [was] only evil continually.

6 And it repented the LORD that he had made man on the earth, and it grieved him at his heart.

In these text, the word heart is defined as: ***inner man, mind, will, understanding, the inner part or deepest existence; meaning soul or emotions of the heart, or in the midst.*** The deepest part of man was evil. His mind, will, soul and emotions were all evil. This evil ran so deep that it grieved God in His heart. Who would think that the greatest creation of God's hand would become so deeply rooted with evil. I was in study while writing this book and God revealed to me that, such deeply rooted sin came from a deep root of power. The greater the power, the greater the fall of sin.

Ezekiel 28:13 Thou hast been in Eden the garden of God; every precious stone [was] thy covering, the sardius, topaz, and the diamond, the beryl, the onyx, and the jasper, the sapphire, the emerald, and the carbuncle, and gold: the workmanship of thy tabrets and of thy pipes was prepared in thee in the day that thou wast created.

14 Thou [art] the anointed cherub that covereth; and I have set thee [so]: thou wast upon the holy mountain of God; thou hast walked up and down in the midst of the stones of fire.

15 Thou [wast] perfect in thy ways from the day that thou wast created, till iniquity was found in thee.

16 By the multitude of thy merchandise they have filled the midst of thee with violence, and thou hast sinned: therefore I will cast thee as profane out of the mountain of God: and I will destroy thee, O covering cherub, from the midst of the stones of fire.

17 Thine heart was lifted up because of thy beauty, thou hast corrupted thy wisdom by reason of thy brightness: I will cast thee to the ground, I will lay thee before kings, that they may behold thee.

Isaiah 14:12 How art thou fallen from heaven, O Lucifer, son of the morning! [how] art thou cut down to the ground, which didst weaken the nations!

13 For thou hast said in thine heart, I will ascend into heaven, I will exalt my throne above the stars of God: I will sit also upon the mount of the congregation, in the sides of the north:

14 I will ascend above the heights of the clouds; I will be like the most High.

Ezekiel explains that satan was an angel. Every precious stone was in him. Verse fourteen says that he was anointed and verse fifteen said he was perfect in his ways. Imagine satan being perfect in all his ways. Then iniquity was found in him. Isaiah picks up the story and says, how did you fall O lucifer? How did you lose such a position? It started in his heart. Verse thirteen of Isaiah says, "for thou has said in thine heart". God's anointed angel fell from grace. Created with such beauty and perfection, he fell due to an imagination of the heart. This caused satan's great down fall. Ezekiel says "Thine heart was lifted up because of thy beauty"(v17). Satan knew his power and beauty. He understood his importance and authority. He was an angel created to usher in the presence of God. His authority was to bring heaven into a kneeling position of worship. He later asked Jesus himself to kneel and worship him, (Matthew 4:8-10). His desire to be praised like God prompted his down fall. Man's fall was in this same way, desiring to have knowledge and wisdom.

Genesis 3:5 For God doth know that in the day ye eat thereof, then your eyes shall be opened, and ye shall be as gods, knowing good and evil.

6 And when the woman saw that the tree [was] good for food, and that it [was] pleasant to the eyes, and a tree to be desired to make [one] wise, she took of the fruit thereof, and did eat, and gave also unto her husband with her; and he did eat.

The serpent placed before Eve the imagination of being like God. The same image he chased in his fall. The woman saw that the tree was pleasant and could make one wise, so she took it. Eve saw the authority in the fruit, not the evil of her choice. The image he placed before her birthed a desire of evil in her heart. This evil would carry on in the woman's seed continually.

Genesis 8:21 And the LORD smelled a sweet savour; and the LORD said in his heart, I will not again curse the ground any more for man's sake; for the imagination of man's heart [is] evil from his youth; neither will I again smite any more every thing living, as I have done.

God said the imagination of man's heart is evil from his youth or childhood. This is the second time in scripture that man's heart was mentioned in reference with the imagination of it. This time The Lord says, I know mans heart is evil from birth. From the beginning man will seek evil in his heart. From as early as our youth we'll find a way to imagine evil against God. Free will, is now the authority driving us away from God's heart. It is the power of our free will that has us so far away. This same power has driven us out of our rightful places with God, and into the hands of the enemy. All of this is due to inner imaginations of evil.

Imagination is defined as: images formed by the mental, that is not perceived as real.

Both satan and Eve had an imagination of having all power and gaining a ton of wisdom. This was a perception that cannot be perceived as real. To have all power, was an imagination that could never be possible, with a heart full of evil and disobedience. This image could not possibly happen, seeing that God will forever be the creator, and nothing could ever replace that. It is up to us to recognize this evil and change the direction of our hearts. Let us all chase not after our authority but, after the heart of God. Amen!

Restoring our hearts to God: Chapter 2 Knowing your heart.

Psalm 4:2,4 O ye sons of men, how long [will ye turn] my glory into shame? [how long] will ye love vanity, [and] seek after leasing? Selah. 4 Stand in awe, and sin not: commune with your own heart upon your bed, and be still. Selah.

God first asked the question, how long will ye turn my glory into shame? This question would stand as a testament to man. Indicating that his glory was being defiled. Not only was it being defiled, it was being betrayed by mans heart. The glory was being made powerless by mans evil imaginations. Man would begin to follow the evil of his heart, displaying all wickedness. This would lead to God's conversation with man, about his heart. Verse four says commune with your own heart. This statement is expressed to us to search our will, motives and desires daily. To search the darkness of it. The word commune means, *to communicate intimately with*. When God said communicate intimately with your heart, this was a petition to seek the most inner parts of our heart and know them. It was a call to really seek our hearts.

Jeremiah 17: 9 The heart [is] deceitful above all [things], and desperately wicked: who can know it?

10 I the LORD search the heart, [I] try the reins, even to give every man according to his ways, [and] according to the fruit of his doings.

God said the heart is deceitful above "*All*" things. I hear so many times people say, "the Lord knows my heart." And their right. It's deceitful, and not only deceitful but "desperately wicked." This statement continues the outline in chapter one, mans heart is evil continually, by the imaginations of it. By communing with the heart we can identify some of our evil intentions. Had Peter communed with his heart before he told Jesus he would never deny him, he probably would've kept silent. We sometimes speak before we think in dealing with God. We make promises like, "Lord if you get me out of this I'll never do it again." Lies. We end up back in the same boat with no paddle. How could you promise to never sin against God again? You don't even know your heart to promise such a thing. David prayed an awesome prayer in Psalms 139.

Psalms 139: 23 Search me, O God, and know my heart: try me, and know my thoughts:

24 And see if [there be any] wicked way in me, and lead me in the way everlasting.

In Jeremiah God said, "I search the heart". David said in Psalms, "search me, and know my heart." He also asked God to show it to him. How many of us really want God to search our heart? David wanted God to not only search his heart, but correct it, "and lead me in the way everlasting." This came from David realizing he didn't know the heart. After seeing his actions over and over again, he cried out for assistance. We need to take up this same format of prayer in an attempt to restore our heart to the King. Let God's word be a light to our heart so it can shine on the darkness within it. I urge us all to examine our hearts daily in our course of life. In Jesus name Amen.

Restoring our hearts to God: Chapter 3 Requirements of the heart.

Matthew 15:7 [Ye] hypocrites, well did Esaias prophesy of you, saying,

8 This people draweth nigh unto me with their mouth, and honoureth me with [their] lips; but their heart is far from me.

9 But in vain they do worship me, teaching [for] doctrines the commandments of men.

The first thing Jesus says after he criticizes their heart is, "in vain they do worship me". One of the reasons our heart was created, was to worship. Worship is a reverence. It's an extreme obedience to the will of God. Jesus explains, that the people give many honors with their mouth, but the heart has yet to follow. It is a command to worship God in our entire being. All God really want is a relationship with his people. Most people look at worship as being controlled or some form of slavery. It's a commitment to trust God with our entire being.

Deuteronomy 6:5 And thou shalt love the LORD thy God with all thine heart, and with all thy soul, and with all thy might.

God commanded that we love him with our whole heart. This is the only true way to worship. Matthew 15:9 again says, "in vain they do worship me". In other words, they had a form of worship but it wasn't in sincerity. It didn't have the passion of their hearts behind it. They were teaching and preaching but with no passion. They knew the word and excelled in it, but just refused to release their hearts.

Psalms 12:2 They speak vanity every one with his neighbor: [with] flattering lips [and] with a double heart do they speak.

Knowing the word but refusing to surrender is just like having that double heart. We tend to speak the word when it benefits us but never use it as a lifestyle. There is no connection with the actions of our hearts and the words of our mouth. There's no sincerity in our lives to connect the two. There's not even a desire in our lives to connect the two. If we just have to render one of the two to God, it shall very well be our hearts rather than our mouths.

Proverbs 10:20 The tongue of the just [is as] choice silver: the heart of the wicked [is] little worth.

The heart of the wicked has a little worth. Wow! When the word of God meets the obedience of our hearts, it produces power. Without obedience there is no power. Again, worship is extreme obedience. It's the giving up of our hearts. We have so much connected to our hearts that it's almost impossible to release our hearts to God. Releasing our hearts is the ultimate way of trusting him.

Proverbs 3:5 Trust in the LORD with all thine heart; and lean not unto thine own understanding.

The only way to give up your heart, is to trust in Him. Jesus Said, those who worship "*Must*" worship in spirit and truth, John 4:24. In other words you have to submit your life. You have to live the reality of your words. You must give your heart back to the father. In doing this He purifies it, cleansing all evil and making it valuable again. Lets give God our whole heart and become valuable in the kingdom of God again. Adding to his glory our availability and sincerity. Reaching the throne with extreme obedience and undefiled worship. Matching the power with truth, (the reality of our words, and the obedience of our lives). Let the restoration begin in Jesus name. Amen!

Restoring our hearts to God: Chapter 4 Guarding your heart.

Proverbs 4:23 Keep thy heart with all diligence; for out of it [are] the issues of life.

Psalms 7:9 Oh let the wickedness of the wicked come to an end; but establish the just: for the righteous God trieth the hearts and reins.

10 My defence [is] of God, which saveth the upright in heart.

The scripture tells us to keep our heart with **"ALL DILIGENCE."** That word diligence means ***careful and persistent effort***. In your heart are the issues of life. Psalms seven, David says let the wickedness end; but establish the just. David was ready for the wickedness to end in his life. He was willing to submit all of his heart to the father. Verse 10 he announces the father as his defense. Knowing the issues he had in life, he decided to shift the responsibility of guarding his heart by putting it in the safety of the father. There's no better place than The Lord's hand for your heart. In order to protect it ourselves we must renew our heart in the word daily. We must be careful and persistent with it. We must treat it like the precious treasure box it was created as. We have to break open the box of our heart daily, through consistent and sincere worship. Presenting it a treasure back unto God. Wouldn't it be awesome to bow before The Lord opening our hearts to him, knowing that he will protect the treasures of it? It is important to watch what we keep around our heart. The atmosphere of our heart must be pleasant enough for God's spirit to come in. Most of the time we have to many distractions around us to effectively guard our hearts.

Joshua 22:5 But take diligent heed to do the commandment and the law, which Moses the servant of the LORD charged you, to love the LORD your God, and to walk in all his ways, and to keep his commandments, and to cleave unto him, and to serve him with all your heart and with all your soul.

Joshua told us to take diligent heed to the commandment, cleave to him and serve him. This is the key part, with all your heart and all your soul. Where your heart is, trust your soul is not too far away. It was Joshua's goal to have us cleave to God with our heart and soul. This is the process to diligently keeping our hearts.

To cleave means to: to stick to, to hang on to, and to overtake.

Joshua wanted us to hang on to and overtake God with our hearts and soul. This is our way of worship. It is our way of saying, I trust in you my King. It keeps us in his face, and stuck to his will. Take heed to this message and guard the atmosphere of your heart with careful and persistent measures. That means I have to watch the measure of company I keep. It also means don't subject yourself to anything unpleasant to God. The atmosphere around our heart must be totally clear before God. For most of us our treasure boxes must be empty. Some of us have too many ungodly influences around our hearts, causing it to be impossible for the blood to flow through it. The number one cause for a heart attack, is blocked arteries. Like so we have spiritual heart attacks, causing harsh and unusual pain, shortness of breath and dizziness.

- The unusual pain comes from an blocked artery, which hurts when the blood can't flow through when faced with trials and hardships. That artery can be prayer, fasting or reading. When distractions are evident and we don't handle them we are subject to a heart attack.

- Shortness of breath means, we can't experience the freshness of Gods spirit. When life seems like its being choked out of us, we may be suffering from a spiritual heart attack. This hinders hearing God, or experiencing new revelation from God.
- Dizziness means confusion of the heart. The word says a double minded man is unstable in "***all***" his ways (James 1:8). We can not try to live Godly and ungodly at the same time, it causes a life of dizziness/confusion. It disables you to be well balanced.

All of these heart attack symptoms are dangerous and extremely hazardous to the body (The Church). We must at all cost avoid this spiritual heart attack. To avoid these attacks we must first eat right and exercise daily, (meaning reading & living the word). We must put the word into us daily. Man does not eat from bread alone but every word that proceeds from the mouth of God, Matthew 4:4. This is the true and only way to guard our hearts from the attacks of the enemy. I pray the power and strength of God. Amen!

Restoring Our Hearts To God: Chapter 5 Distance of the Heart

Matthew 15:8 This people draweth nigh unto me with their mouth, and honoureth me with [their] lips; but their heart is far from me.

Jesus stated this in a testimony against a sinful and rebellious nation. In this statement he projects the distance of the mouth as being close and the the heart not close enough. God is not impressed with our many words and crafty philosophies. He desires our hearts to be the same place our treasures rest. God is too big to be involved with our little images of worship. I once saw a statement "don't measure success on cars and clothes." These items have become an new form of worship. We honor God with the foolish praise of thanks for an item that has our heart instead of him possessing it. Lord thank you for this car, thank you for this job, thank you for this house. In reality all of these things are higher priority than God in our lives. You get close with your mouth, but where is your heart? Thank him for the healing, but continue the unhealthy lifestyle. Praise him for the deliverance, but go back to the issues. How far is your heart? Too often we become deceived by the desperately wickedness of our heart.

Jeremiah 17:9 The heart [is] deceitful above all [things], and desperately wicked: who can know it?

Deceitful above "*All*" things. We think that God get tickled about our lip service. Not so. That's why so many of us willfully disobey The Lord, and then think that we can easily just walk back into his presence. So not true. See the presence of God was never meant to be taken lightly. We were to cherish the fact that he allowed us in his presence.

Psalms 22:3 But thou [art] holy, [O thou] that inhabitest the praises of Israel.

David in this scripture tells us that God lives in the praises of Israel, but that doesn't mean he honored them. What that explains is they consistently spoke of him. The children of Israel loved to speak highly of God when they needed him. This was the same nation that wanted a king (Saul) over God. The same nation that asked Moses why did God bring us here to die? God did live in there praises again that just simply mean they loved to talk about him. My question is, where is your hearts? When will there be a nation that not only speak to God but service him with their hearts? When will there be a people that not only praise God for his many gifts, but honor him with them as well? In other words don't just praise him for the gift, but be a blessing to someone else through the gift. This chapter is simply a reminder it's not about our words it's about our service. It's about not only telling God I love you but actually showing him. Sacrifice for your King. Both in lip service as well as heart dedication. There's a song writer that says,

"I'm tired of telling you, you have me when I know you really don't. I'm tired of telling you I'll follow, when I know I really won't."

These words are a cry to say, "Lord I'm done talking, I need to show you." How many of you feel like that? Lord I'm tired of empty promises and broken vows. We must press to become equal with our service. Not only will I confess you but I'll live your divine will. Not only will I boast of your praises but, I'll live as an example. We must draw closer to God with our day to day service and dedication. Let's open our hearts and draw closer to our God.

Restoring our hearts to God:
Chapter 6 Conclusion.

In this short message of the heart, I hope you received the strength and knowledge necessary to continue in the blessed glory of God. Below are some key scriptures to help you continue in restoring your heart to the father.

Genesis 6:5 And GOD saw that the wickedness of man [was] great in the earth, and [that] every imagination of the thoughts of his heart [was] only evil continually.

6 And it repented the LORD that he had made man on the earth, and it grieved him at his heart.

Genesis 8:21 And the LORD smelled a sweet savour; and the LORD said in his heart, I will not again curse the ground any more for man's sake; for the imagination of man's heart [is] evil from his youth; neither will I again smite any more every thing living, as I have done.

Psalm 4: 2,4 O ye sons of men, how long [will ye turn] my glory into shame? [how long] will ye love vanity, [and] seek after leasing? Selah. 4 Stand in awe, and sin not: commune with your own heart upon your bed, and be still. Selah.

Jeremiah 17: 9 The heart [is] deceitful above all [things], and desperately wicked: who can know it?

10 I the LORD search the heart, [I] try the reins, even to give every man according to his ways, [and] according to the fruit of his doings.

Psalms 139: 23 Search me, O God, and know my heart: try me, and know my thoughts:

24 And see if [there be any] wicked way in me, and lead me in the way everlasting.

Matthew 15:7 [Ye] hypocrites, well did Esaias prophesy of you, saying,

8 This people draweth nigh unto me with their mouth, and honoureth me with [their] lips; but their heart is far from me.

9 But in vain they do worship me, teaching [for] doctrines the commandments of men.

Deuteronomy 6:5 And thou shalt love the LORD thy God with all thine heart, and with all thy soul, and with all thy might.

Proverbs 10:20 The tongue of the just [is as] choice silver: the heart of the wicked [is] little worth

Proverbs 4:23 Keep thy heart with all diligence; for out of it [are] the issues of life.

Psalms 7:9 Oh let the wickedness of the wicked come to an end; but establish the just: for the righteous God trieth the hearts and reins.

10 My defence [is] of God, which saveth the upright in heart.

PART III

Restoring God's will in your life: Chapter 1 Forfeit of the Will...

Genesis 2:8-9,15-17 8 And the LORD God planted a garden eastward in Eden; and there he put the man whom he had formed.

9 And out of the ground made the LORD God to grow every tree that is pleasant to the sight, and good for food; the tree of life also in the midst of the garden, and the tree of knowledge of good and evil. 15 And the LORD God took the man, and put him into the garden of Eden to dress it and to keep it.

16 And the LORD God commanded the man, saying, Of every tree of the garden thou mayest freely eat:

17 But of the tree of the knowledge of good and evil, thou shalt not eat of it: for in the day that thou eatest thereof thou shalt surely die.

The scriptures explain that God gave Adam a commandment of his divine will. This will was based upon the knowledge God had, along with the plan God had for Adam. It was a will directly from the throne. In life we encounter three types of wills. We have self-will, perfect-will and divine will. Self-will happens when we totally exclude God from our decision making process. Think about it, the bible says "seek ye First" the "kingdom of God" and "His" righteousness Matthew 6:33. Our day-to-day thought process should include the Father. After all he is the "Author" and "Finisher" of our faith Hebrews 12:2. It only makes more sense to ask the author of your faith to tell you what he wrote about you.

Jeremiah 29:11-14 11 For I know the thoughts that I think toward you, saith the LORD, thoughts of peace, and not of evil, to give you an expected end.

12 Then shall ye call upon me, and ye shall go and pray unto me, and I will hearken unto you.

13 And ye shall seek me, and find [me], when ye shall search for me with all your heart.

14 And I will be found of you, saith the LORD: and I will turn away your captivity, and I will gather you from all the nations, and from all the places whither I have driven you, saith the LORD; and I will bring you again into the place whence I caused you to be carried away captive.

God said I know what I'm thinking about you. Call on me and seek me with your whole heart, then will I be found of you and bring you to a blessed place once again. This is the only process to restore us from self-will.

- Self-will becomes a deal breaker with God. It actually shows that, Lord, I really don't need you. Look at all the decisions we make on a day to day basis without God. These choices become the perfect let down or disappointment we run to God to fix later on in life. If we actually took the time to *"Seek Him First"*, our lives would run a lot smoother.

- Perfect-will is God's ability to turn what's imperfect into a desired blessing. When you look at the story of Ishmael or David, it shows God's mercy upon these imperfect situations. With Ishmael, he was not the divine will of God for Abraham, but God perfected it and made him, (Ishmael) a great nation. With David the mighty warrior. One who had many imperfections. God allowed a throne which Christ is seated on. God took these imperfections and made them to be great possibilities, with the progressive process of submitting to His will. In other words, God's everlasting love can perfect your mistake, if you allow Him to. You must yield yourself to His will. We are the perfected will of God. Born into sin, shaped in iniquity, perfected by His blood and saved through our confession and believing in our hearts. Adam with self will, lost his rights to everlasting life. The creative design to live forever was forfeited by going against God's command. This would destroy human life as we know it and God's purpose for all man kind.

God, perfecting Adam's self-will, came up with a plan through Christ to project His divine will and everlasting life.

- Divine will is simply, his original plan for your life. It is a direct plan or purpose from heaven. Seeing that Adam lost the will in a garden, God sent sent Jesus into a garden to regain it **Genesis 3:1-8, Matthew 26:38-44.** God strategically planned the regain of His will through Jesus submitting in the garden. The same place the first man lost it, would be the same atmosphere the savior regained it. Not only did Adam lose his will, he lost his alpha right. Jesus submitting to the divine will gave him the title *"Alpha"* meaning first, **Revelation 1:8,11; 21:6; 22:13.** Now through Jesus (who became the divine will in the flesh), we have the opportunity to receive the divine will of Adam. Eternal life.

1st Corinthians 15:21-22 (21) For since by man [came] death, by man [came] also the resurrection of the dead.

(22) For as in Adam all die, even so in Christ shall all be made alive.

We must now accept the divine will over our lives by the simple, but yet challenging decision to surrender in our garden of faith. We have a great opportunity to live God's will in the fullness of health, prosperity, joy and peace that surpasses all understanding. This is all found in God's divine will. Jesus prayed, "Let your will be done on earth as it is in heaven". That prayer was prompted as an example for us to pray. Look at the power in it. Jesus asked for the will of heaven to be done. There's no greater will we can choose in life, other than heavens will. If we consider what goes on in heaven, the worship, the admiration and reverence of God it only makes sense to pray this will. To stand in awe of The Lord and the beauty of his holiness. To follow every command of worship. This is the divine will of God. If we just thrust for this and surrender in our garden, then we'll walk in the fresh blessings of our king. Amen.

Restoring God's will in your life: Chapter 2 Choices in the garden.

Matthew 26:36-39, (36) Then cometh Jesus with them unto a place called Gethsemane, and saith unto the disciples, Sit ye here, while I go and pray yonder.

37 And he took with him Peter and the two sons of Zebedee, and began to be sorrowful and very heavy.

38 Then saith he unto them, My soul is exceeding sorrowful, even unto death: tarry ye here, and watch with me.

39 And he went a little further, and fell on his face, and prayed, saying, O my Father, if it be possible, let this cup pass from me: nevertheless not as I will, but as thou [wilt].

Gethsemane is defined as *"an oil press"* in the Greek language. The oil press was used to produce the precious oil used for anointing. This press applied several hundred pounds of pressure to the olives just to produce. A whole tree sometimes produced only five liters of oil. As precious as it is the olive is extremely bitter, and virtually inedible. Symbolically this garden was used to produce the precious anointing of Jesus for our will. The thought of taking on several hundred pounds of sin crushed the virgin olive, Jesus. The living tree of life produced so little sweat, but every drop covered a multitude of sins. Just like the olive, our sins are extremely bitter, and inedible, but Jesus endured them all. It was at this moment, in the middle of this garden that Jesus made a decision to obey the divine will of God. The oil press created such an intense atmosphere to decide in, that it caused the master to sweat from that pressure. Jesus starts off arriving in a sorrowful and heavy state. He describes His feelings as *"exceeding sorrowful".* These emotions promoted a prayer in attempt to alter the divine will of God. *"O my Father, if it be possible, let this cup pass from me".* Many of us have been under some type of sorrowful, heavy pressure. This is our oil pressing process. Biblically the oil represented the anointing of God. In this case God was after something greater than oil. Something that could seal the deal on this divine will. He was after the blood. The precious, uncontaminated blood of Jesus. The bible says that our savior sweated drops of blood, from deciding to follow the will.

Luke <u>22:44</u> And being in an agony he prayed more earnestly: and his sweat was as it were great drops of blood falling down to the ground.

Luke describes this experience as *"agony"*. These feelings crushed the very soul of Christ, releasing the all powerful blood of Christ over God's will. This allowed man to have power over his will again and make us joint heirs to the throne. Jesus chose to pass on his own fleshly desire to fulfill God's divine will. In doing so He was given a name above all names, and power over all things. Adam's decision was quite different. Eden on the other hand means *"pleasure"*. Adam was in a beautiful place when he decided to fall. Knowing God's divine will, he chose pleasure. It is God's desire to have us choose His will right in the midst of our pleasure. It is in our most desirable stages of life, evil is present waiting to present your self-will. Look at the fall of Adam and Eve. Adam and Eve chose the provision, beauty, wisdom and authority in a piece of fruit, verses the same attributes in God. Jesus chose the crushing agony of sorrow and heaviness, knowing that this would produce a greater avenue of life. By denying pleasure, Adam could've changed his whole destiny. Instead he destroyed an ultimate connection of grace and power over his life. By choosing the oil press we give God his just due in our lives. Think about it. The oil represents the anointing. So the more the oil press crushes you the more the anointing is produced. Unlike Jesus, we can't take the crushing process. Our desires sometimes block us from surrendering to God's divine will. We just can't handle it. That's why we generally end up choosing our will. If we can just loose our will (life), it would allow God to bring out of us the most holiest, purest form in us. We all should allow this crushing process in order to sustain the blessings of God.

Restoring God's will in your life: Chapter 3 The weight of you decision..

Genesis 3:13-19 13 And the LORD God said unto the woman, What [is] this [that] thou hast done? And the woman said, The serpent beguiled me, and I did eat.

14 And the LORD God said unto the serpent, Because thou hast done this, thou [art] cursed above all cattle, and above every beast of the field; upon thy belly shalt thou go, and dust shalt thou eat all the days of thy life:

15 And I will put enmity between thee and the woman, and between thy seed and her seed; it shall bruise thy head, and thou shalt bruise his heel.

16 Unto the woman he said, I will greatly multiply thy sorrow and thy conception; in sorrow thou shalt bring forth children; and thy desire [shall be] to thy husband, and he shall rule over thee.

17 And unto Adam he said, Because thou hast hearkened unto the voice of thy wife, and hast eaten of the tree, of

which I commanded thee, saying, Thou shalt not eat of it: cursed [is] the ground for thy sake; in sorrow shalt thou eat [of] it all the days of thy life;

18 Thorns also and thistles shall it bring forth to thee; and thou shalt eat the herb of the field;

19 In the sweat of thy face shalt thou eat bread, till thou return unto the ground; for out of it wast thou taken: for dust thou [art], and unto dust shalt thou return.

Adam, Eve and the serpent all chose to disobey the will of the father, resulting in a curse. Self-will was punished by measure of a curse. These curses altered the course of their lives. The serpent was punished to eat dirt all of his life, with a seed that would never have victory. Unto the woman, painful child birth and an inferior feeling toward her husband. The man, hard work and labor was to be his curse, along with a cursed ground. The serpent chose his will of manipulation, coupled with deception. We all know that satan was kicked out of heaven. His lust for power and control, caused him to lose his position in the presence of the king. Adam and Eve's choice was similar, resulting in them being kicked out of Eden. The place called "pleasure." They were cast away from the presence of God based upon their actions. The weight of their decision was costly. Losing the precious ability of having a moment with the king. Likewise we are in the same position. Self-will causes us to forfeit that presence. It takes us out of glory. Think about it, most of the time we choose our will we usually end up in sin, which prohibits us from coming into the King's presence. Sin without repentance is dangerous. We fall short and God forgives. Having no remorse or conviction is the deal breaker. Neither, the serpent nor Adam and Eve repented. The serpent never spoke, and the man and woman blamed others for their faults. With God's divine will there is no excuses. You either follow it or you don't. Not following the will of God is sin. God has a divine will for your life, and its end is promising. With a repenting heart, God can fix your mistake and make it a perfect will. Let us all judge the weight of our will, and turn our hearts back toward God, to restore these broken wills.

Jesus on the other hand, made a decision to go against the pleasurable way out. He chose a more weightier way. He chose the pressing way. The more sorrowful and annoying way. He chose death. Dying to the option of having a will. The gospel says he humbled himself even unto death Philippians 2:8. In doing this He gained *"ALL"* power. Giving man victory in recovering God's divine will in our life. Where we were once defeated we can now proclaim victory! Activate it now. Where there's sickness say, divine healing Isaiah 53:5. Poverty, divine prosperity 3rd John 1:2. Defeat, divine victory Romans 8:37. Every evil work, divine power Luke 10:19. Whatever your issue is God has a divine will for it, and his perfected will has already bridged the gap between the two. You "can do all things" through Christ Philippians 4:13. Seek God, and turn your heart, and watch the divine will manifest itself in your life. Blessed be the will of our father, Amen!

Restoring God's will in your life: Chapter 4 The challenge of God's will.

Matthew 10:38-39 38 And he that taketh not his cross, and followeth after me, is not worthy of me.

39 He that findeth his life shall lose it: and he that loseth his life for my sake shall find it.

Jesus explains in this text that you must take up your cross and follow after Him, in order to be counted worthy of Him. What this literally means is that, Jesus is the will of God and the cross is the way to the will. This cross is the challenge to us all. Jesus hung on the cross in the midst of two thieves as an example of how the cross meets the will in completion to salvation. One of the thieves stated, that he justly received what was due unto him, Luke 23:39-43. In admitting to his wrong doing and excepting his cross Jesus replied, "*To day shalt thou be with me in paradise".* It is this challenge to take up our cross and allow our will to die on the cross, so the will of the father can live. Even while on the cross Jesus cried out asking God, why did you leave me Mark 15:34. This statement lets us know that Jesus' will was dying to God's divine will. The agony He felt in the garden was now surfacing on the cross. This time it would die once and for all. There would be no more questions, just a dying will. The blood that was shed on the cross sealed the deal on our dying will. It set a seal that when we except this challenge to deny our will and take up our cross we become worthy. The blood covers us, stamping us as worthy. Worthy of all of God's will. We're now worthy of healing, prosperity, deliverance, joy, peace, you name it. Your now worthy. Your cross has made you worthy. The divine will of the father meets us right at the cross and extends his hand to receive us.

Luke 23:46 And when Jesus had cried with a loud voice, he said, Father, into thy hands I commend my spirit: and having said thus, he gave up the ghost.

God's hands came down to receive his son. God is asking us to put our will on that cross so that His hands can receive us. Put your life's treasure on your cross. Jesus said, "**He that findeth his life shall lose it: and he that loseth his life for my sake shall find it**". Finding your life is exploring your will. All of your pleasure is required on the cross, this is what makes you worthy. Put what you think should live on the cross. If it was meant to be it will be raised again. Put that relationship on the cross. That house on the cross. Your job on the cross. Every decision in life need to meet the cross first. This is how you lose your life for Christ and find God's will for your life. The moment we put our pleasure on the cross and ask for His hands, He receives us. We need to do this daily. Every day we should surrender our will on the cross saying, "Lord here's my will now send your hands". The same Christ who gave up the ghost, was raised from the dead. The blessed part about that was, wherever He didn't have power, He got up with it. In other words. When you put your will on the cross and it dyes, then God raises you up in a will that can't be defeated. You gain a whole new will that can't be stopped. Let the hand of God come receive you now, by stretching your arms and fastening your feet saying, "into your hands I commend my spirit". The enemy didn't know that when he put the nails into our Lord while in this position, he fastened Him into a surrendering position. He couldn't run from the will. Likewise we need to fasten ourselves on our cross and receive the will. The nail in the hands symbolizes the victory in whatever we touch according to divine will. The nails in the feet symbolizes victory in wherever our feet goes, Joshua 1:3 Every place that the sole of your foot shall tread upon, that have I given unto you, as I said unto Moses. Let us surrender our will now, only to be held by our King as we fasten ourself to the cross and receive God's divine will. Amen!

Restoring God's will in your life: Chapter 5 Victory

Matthew 28:18 And Jesus came and spake unto them, saying, All power is given unto me in heaven and in earth.

2nd Peter 1:3 According as his divine power hath given unto us all things that [pertain] unto life and godliness, through the knowledge of him that hath called us to glory and virtue:

Jesus says in Matthew he was given all power. That power had authority in heaven and in earth. 2nd Peter explains, his divine power has given us *"All things"*, pertaining to life and godliness. The later clause of the scripture says we've been called to glory and virtue. That same virtue gave us victory. Not only victory on earth but in heaven as well. With that virtue everything that pertains to life, I conquer, everything that pertains to godliness I have. When we realize God's divine will it unlocks a whole new life and authority in us, to walk in the victory we were called to.

Matthew 16:19 And I will give unto thee the keys of the kingdom of heaven: and whatsoever thou shalt bind on earth shall be bound in heaven: and whatsoever thou shalt loose on earth shall be loosed in heaven.

Jesus told the disciples after Peter recognized his divine authority and will, you now have keys to the kingdom of heaven. Those keys unlocked the power of heaven, that whatever we loose or bind, God honors. Luke 10:19 says we have power *"over all the power"* of the enemy. Romans 8:37 say we are *"more"* than conquers. This authority is the divine will of God for us to walk in victory. Again 2nd Peter called it His divine power, and we are to obtain it. God has a power that only heaven has seen and it's waiting to be released. It's a perfect power. One that will destroy *"ALL"* wickedness on earth and in high places. We have access to a divine power. It's in His plans for us to live in this power. Picture living life in constant victory. This is not a dream nor ordinary vision, this is the life God chose for us. Genesis 1:26 God said let them have dominion over *"all"* the earth. Every thing that has been created God said man has authority over it. Sickness, I have authority over it. Lack, I have authority over it. Every plan of satan, I have authority over it. Deuteronomy 8:18 God even gives us the power to get wealth. It is the ultimate plan of God for us to have power, and have it divinely. The power is waiting for us to surrender to God's divine will. I pray, by the authority of Christ that we take this potential of power and live on in victory. Let us be blessed in Jesus name. Amen!

REFLECTIONS

REFLECTIONS

REFLECTIONS

REFLECTIONS

About the Author

Charles White is an author that uses unique and challenging topics to expand the mind of his readers. Charles started in ministry over ten years ago as youth pastor of a growing congregation in the city of Detroit. He eventually ventured off to answer his calling as an Elder in a local assembly, and became very active in the community.